Light Frames the Forest

Prayer & Poetry

Light Frames the Forest

S.C. Watson

Copyrighted Material

Light Frames the Forest

Copyright © 2025 by Baja Bad Press, LLC. All Rights Reserved.

No part of this publication may be reproduced, stored in a retrieval system or transmitted, in any form or by any means—electronic, mechanical, photocopying, recording, or otherwise—without prior written permission from the publisher, except for the inclusion of brief quotations in a review.

For information about this title or to order other books and/or electronic media, contact the publisher:

Baja Bad Press, LLC
bajabadpress@gmail.com

ISBNs:
978-1-7346376-6-3 (hardcover)
978-1-7346376-7-0 (softcover)
978-1-7346376-8-7 (eBook)

Printed in the United States of America

Cover and Interior design: 1106 Design
Cover Art and Illustrations: Andréa Watson

*For our children
and all who embrace light*

Contents

Preface	ix
A Temple in the Wood	3
Prayer and Poetry	7
The Spirits of Trees	10
A Moment in the Redwood Forest	12
The Veil	15
Daystar	17
The Wharf	18
Our Light Hermitage	22
Emily	27
Birth, Our Birth	34
Hear Him	35
The Fisher King's Dream	38
Qumran	44

Omphalós	47
In the Garden	49
Elementum	53
Circumference	57
Father Christmas	66
Fool's Gold	69
Quietus Est	77
My Apocalypse	82
The By and By	88
Of Light and Life	90
Huck's Psalm	93
Luces Peruanas	96
The Nazca Lines	97
Sun Gems	98
Liahona: Light of Paracas?	99
About the Author	103

Preface

Prayer, poetry, and contemplative meditation are spiritually uplifting conduits for light and inspiration, even personal revelation.

The etymology of the word poem is the Latin *poema*, a composition in verse, from the Greek *poēma*, creation. Poets create, and their finest compositions are sacred meditations, heartfelt prayers.

Like prayer, writing is a quiet, reflective pursuit. I write what I want to read; I appreciate poetry and prose that move me.

Enduring poetry conveys truth through emotive, thought-provoking ideas and images. While there are many elements that may be part of a meaningful poem, I focus on five: theme, imagery, symbolism, sound, and structure. Poets understand that every word, every combination of words, matters.

The poet-king David wrote, "The words of the Lord are pure words." (Psalm 12:6, KJV) May we seek to read, ponder, and write pure words, always.

The universe is a place;
truth is a person, even God.

Light frames the forest,

mindful of each sparrow's fall:

springtime's reckoning

A Temple in the Wood

I sense a temple in the wood;
I walk it on the mount.
Its veil billows in the leaves;
a dove drinks from its fount.

Moonlight christens mossy stones,
nature's dewy diadem;
still waters mirror treetop spires'
ascension into heaven.

I see an angel in the clouds;
the stars belie my doubt.
I sense a temple in the wood;
I walk it on the mount.

Sometimes understanding truth requires a simple shift in paradigms; other times, it simply requires faith.

Truth distills like mist:

dewdrops of inspiration

from fountains of light

Words are all we need of truth,

and all we know of light.

Prayer & Poetry

(a meditation)

Who is He?
Do I know Him?
Do my words glorify Him?

I read, write, ponder, and pray.

Who are they?
Do they know Him?
Do I see them as He sees them?

Too many wander,
lost in the world's umbrae.

Who am I?
Does He know me?
Will He call me His friend?

I love, worship, serve, and obey.

All living things have spirits, or intelligence;

life is both temporal and spiritual.

The Spirits of Trees

Dusk denies the forest,
autumn grips the breeze.
Fog cloaks threadbare willows;
songs touch the spirits of trees.

Silence takes the thicket,
fallen flowers freeze.
Ice shapes stony creek beds;
thoughts see the spirits of trees.

Snow betrays the mountain,
winter shrouds the leaves.
Death below the ridgeline—
prayers free the spirits of trees.

*Prayer elevates our individual and collective
spiritual sensibilities,
as God reveals His divine will.*

*Poetry arouses the hopes of passionate hearts,
stirs the dreams of intuitive minds.*

A Moment in the Redwood Forest

(beneath three, towering primeval plants)

He touched the ancient tree
and shut his pale blue eyes.

A spirited pod of gray whales whistled and sang
on the sapphire morning sea.

> "Father, the trees are speaking."
> "What are they saying, Enoch?"
> "They are one, the keepers of the records of the
>   earth. For centuries they've watched, but little
>   time remains."
> "Time? Time for what, son?"
> "Charity. Compassion. Self-control."
> (Or so echoed the distant thunder.)

A shadowy conspiracy of ravens squawked and croaked
above the crisp evening coast.

I closed my heavy eyes
and bowed my head to heaven.

He rarely spoke,
and now, a dire denouement.

Shine forth upon me,

constellation of God's love:

wondrous Tree of Life

The Veil

Silent prayers on an obsidian sea,
a still betwixt troubled, angry sets of waves—
the pale ghost moon's poetry,
scribed in kelp beneath purple depths;
all is vanity.

Above, a cloud of witnesses,
seabirds (or angels),
sings the song that passes understanding;
below, one will know death,
the other, isolation.

Wind whispers across the swells,
a veil of foam kisses my burnt, chafed cheeks;
torrents of water wipe me away.

I close my eyes to see, as night embraces day,
and death, my second birth;
millennia, measured in moments—

Oh, parted shroud between God and Earth!

Daystar

Daystar, my compass be,
truth's upward clarion call;
as I navigate sargassum seas,
illuminate my soul.

The Wharf

The dark scent of smoked fish
meanders up through
adobe shafts and stone chimneys,
up damp corridors
where virescent moss clings
to rusted iron gratings—

I load the cargo deck and curse
the smell of salt and tuna blood
and tired, dingy, rotting berths

and curse the heavy seabirds' call
and silent schooners now beyond
the purple stone marina wall

and curse the lonely chill of dawn,
the charcoal haze across the bay,
and then move on—

The dark scent of smoked fish
streams high into the lazy night.
A dim light from the boathouse
warns of jagged rocks ahead.

Up into the cadaver-blue fog
wanders the gray stream,
vanishing.

Midday sun glistens

through a million particles,

christening the waves

*Study both classical and modern literature;
read from primary sources.
Libraries are wellsprings of creativity.*

Write from a place of inspired imagination.

Our Light Hermitage

Stars glide upon wings of light;
shafts of energy,
brilliant white trails,
spill across space.
Light speaks to our spirits—
a still, small voice whispers
quiet, contemplative peace.

The moon drifts upon tides of light;
wave against wave,
knowledge floods fallen shores,
pools of pure intelligence.
Light illuminates our countenances—
its glow awakens our minds,
softens our hearts, transforms our souls.

Earth spins upon rings of light;
by conscious choice
we dwell in a light hermitage,
an azure sea of opaque glass.
Light flows from a source eternal—
a circle of oneness embraces us,
His defining light, the light of truth.

Poets are instruments of truth;

their light sounds in shadows,

cries out from dark spaces.

The written word is the single most effective means of communicating thought over time and space.

Poetry is beauty, and beauty is truth, absolute truth; we seek after it.

Be a student of poetry; let your unique angel voice forever resound in the poetic firmament.

To write is to create, and creation is divine.

EMILY

To savor but a moment
alone with her verse
is to taste time eternal.

*(Emily Dickinson viewed God and his kingdom as the
Circumference. Hers was an angel voice.)*

LIGHT FRAMES THE FOREST

When friends are poets

their shared light is amplified.

Cosmology's core,

creation's Circumference:

Concentric circles

"*My business is circumference.*"
Emily Dickinson, April 16, 1862

Ethereal light

penetrates coal firmament,

reveals bright new orb

The Star became the Light;

the Lamb became the Shepherd.

And the Shepherd is the Light of the World.

Nothing is so precious as water in the desert.

Birth, Our Birth

In a simple stable
behind a crowded inn
she humbly bore our Lord,
King of women and men.

Savior of humankind,
He humbly bore our sins
near the brook of Cedron
in an olive garden.

Hear Him

Hear Him knock, lost souls—
Earth's deep valleys shall be filled;
her mountains made low.

Immersed in water,
all righteousness, He fulfilled;
straightway He rose, Lord:

Jesus Christ

White dove descended,
Spirit, upon Him lighted;
the Father praised Him.

Witness of the Light,
all flesh shall see salvation—
hear Him, world; He knocks.

The world's light is temporary and artificial;

the Light of the World is eternal and absolute.

The Fisher King's Dream

"Whom does the Grail serve?"

Wounded Fisher King,
Guardian of the Goblet,
fishes a dead stream
and dreams: rock gardens,
cherry blossoms in spring's breeze,
clear, cool mountain pools.

Soldiers take the field;
archers line stone castle walls.
Burst bright, black powder!
Self-inflicted wound
bleeds blue; equinoctial stars
shroud sepulchral clouds.

Burnt oaken timbers'
ash snows bury gold embers:
famine's dry wasteland.
England's tattered flags
hang like pale, wind-blown corpses;
David's sword shattered.

Perceval arrives,
adorned in silver, bestride
Arthur's white stallion.
Impaled Fisher King,
Guardian of the Hallows,
wakes, and glances up.

His skeletal realm
desolate, dun, war-ravaged;
and he, without heir.

Brave knight dismounts, kneels,
bows his head in sworn respect.
Easter's moon rises,

as the gallant chevalier prays:

"Wounded Fisher King,
Guardian of Christ's Chalice,
whom does the Grail serve?"

*Prayer is a personal portal to the will of God,
a humble conversation with Him.*

*Poetry is a creative reflection of the observations,
experiences, and intelligence of the poet.*

The ancient covenant path is narrow, painfully difficult, and seldom hiked; there are always two ways. That said, I'd rather be at the bottom of the path, ascending, than at the top, descending.

Talons saber-sharp,

breathing the fires of freewill—

we fight like dragons!

Ancient ostraca,

potsherds of poetic thought,

echo from the earth

Qumran

A white Barbary falcon,
imperially perched on a desert precipice,
surveils the sacramental plateau:
hidden terraces riddled with tunnels,
dim passageways where hosts of swallows dwell,
a subterranean sanctuary—
scriptorium of forgotten prophets.

Deep beneath the dry,
lifeless illumination of a lilac sunset,
within smoky, torchlit chambers,
Sons of Light gathered to dance
and repeat the ancient rituals and catacomb truths,
covenants preserved like their polished granite
altars under layers of dust and sand.

Clay vessels, copper plates,
silver basins, and papyrus scrolls
inscribed with eschatological prose,
line the dark halls of Melchizedek.

I pause to rest on the Dead Sea's gritty shore
and ponder the immensity of their temple refuge,
now a distant shadow, a type—
and read their hierocentric declaration:

"THE ABOMINATION OF DESOLATION."

A second death, a spiritual demise, an end of days cometh.

*Seek knowledge,
embrace light,
treasure love,
and glorify God—*

HONOR HIM.

Omphalós

(center or navel)

Celestial spirits
descend through space, quickening
physical bodies

Omphalós

Life's fragile mortals
pass through time's ports, harboring
spiritual souls

To read and write fresh, original poetry is to participate in the great conversation of humankind.

In the Garden

I woke one night beneath a branch
where sweet citrus trees choked the skies;
an ancient corpse with twisted limbs,
budded black primordial lies.

Eve rose to dance, dark mist caressed,
tasted fruit of the sacred tree;
wrapped herself in the serpent's glance,
saw clearly what I could not see.

She brushed my hair with silken hands,
washed my feet in her tears of shame.
Together we scribed holy psalms,
cried hymns of paradise reclaimed.

But that was worlds ago; Earth time,
seven millennia have passed.
I gently take her soul in mine,
and cross vast galaxies of glass.

A still, small voice throbs,

reverberates within me;

heartbeats pulsate, "Faith."

Knowledge is the rational and extrarational recognition, understanding, and acceptance of objective, absolute truth. Light emanates truth; great literature flows from light and knowledge. All light and knowledge issues from Him.

He is truth.

Elementum

Life emanates from His reservoir of intelligence:
slipstream-spirits, children of promise,
funnel through celestial portals and astral conduits
across an ethereal veil of oblivion.

Ephemeral fuselages of dust, brimming with blood,
transitory, clay capsules conceived on an azure planet
beneath starry firmament and amniotic seas,
yearning for the opportunity
to burst free, and squeal.

Waves of black water move upon shifting shores,
aluminum sparkles through plastic tide pools;
spring's smoggy blood moon rises slowly
over shattered shells and splintered driftwood.

But shafts of sunlight pierce the caramel mist,
sparks dissipate the leaden, morning dew;
lightning illuminates an amethyst sky.

An intrepid millennium dawns—
and pillars of fire reveal paradisiacal glory:
a forgotten treasury of light!

The truest path to genuine self-love

passes through simple acts of selfless service.

CIRCUMFERENCE

Daybreak, and I am desperately alone,
forsaken by silent, digital gods.
Electricity pools in grey, concrete gardens,
steel palms line asphalt crops;
the jacaranda trees bloom desert-dry,
skeletal shades of fading amethyst
beneath a dying orb.

Hours pass, and miles;
I mutter empty, dehydrated verse
and stumble to the edge of an ancient abyss,
a deep, spiraling, reptilian cave,
encrusted with trinkets of gold and silver—
bejeweled, cobweb nightmares.

"You can buy anything in this world for money,"
hisses a venomous lizard
(a gnarled, subterranean Gila monster
hidden from view in a shadowy crevice)
through the damp, sulphury vapor—

Jealous, crimson dragon!

Forlorn, I kneel in the scorpion sand
beside a fallen saguaro,
bow low in broken obeisance,
and submit to my Lord.

I utter an anguished prayer of contrition,
gasping for short, shallow breaths
between sorrowful pleas, sanguinary tears;
then slowly, hesitantly, open my eyes.

My heart hears a still, small voice,
a personal, spiritual connection,
invite me to rise;
his loving answer fills my harrowed soul.

I taste the living water,
his forgiveness, a gift of eternal grace—
his light, a promised treasure,
an incandescent endowment of truth.

He takes me by the hand;
his loving embrace holds me, enfolds me,
gently guides me safely home—
At-one-ment,
Circumference.

He shapes my desires;

thus refined by holy fire,

my light burns brighter

Reading cultivates fresh ideas;

journaling preserves them.

Read for inspiration;

write for experience, and recollection.

Ghosts of my journal—

lost thoughts, haunting forgotten pages:

cursed souls

Lucid dreams, scribbled

on scraps of paper napkins:

my last night's poem

The measure of artistic intelligence is diligence.

Father Christmas

"Wassail!" Ol' sleigh thumps—
meggle bump-bump, meggle crump;
bellycheer, kerplunk!

*The spirit of Santa is the spirit of giving,
and of the Light-giver.*

*(This haiku includes a variety of archaic
English words chosen for their onomatopoeia
and various Christmas connotations.)*

When I'm distracted, creativity abandons me.

Writing is my tempestuous remedy for writer's block;

reading is my gentle breeze in silent woods.

Sage saguaro tribes,

arms raised to turquoise heavens:

prayerful desert pleas

Fool's Gold

Dusk's plum clouds over Purgatory
paint savage, crumbling cliffs—
dark serpentine shadows,
slithering across jagged crags;
their mythical souls' empty sarcophagi,
desiccated desert skins
encased in chalky cacti skeletons,
lay dying on the desert.

Vast, silent wasteland of my birth,
buried beneath drifts of rock and sand—
shards of scattered covenants,
forgotten, petroglyph promises,
empty hands washed in crimson clay
imprinted on granite altars
beneath grizzly bears, mule deer, and aliens.
A fiery whirlwind, "El Diablo's Draft,"
whistles through tumbleweed crevices;
mustangs drink from dry, gravel creeks.
Footfalls echo the ancient Skinwalkers:
tales of Cochise, Geronimo, and yesterday,
desperate tribal dances, mystical wolfen figures,
above ritual flutes and drums.

One eternal round—

A sinuous fork appears on the trail,
two ways, but one the smoother worn;
I pause to collect a pebble of shining pyrite
and place the treasure in my leather pouch.
One last swallow of water, a crust of fry bread,
then, humming their traditional chant,
I choose the longer, prickly path home.

Slate-blue kestrels dance

and dive under pogonip,

like autumnal leaves

Rabbit tracks across

white powder, disappear like

Indian summer

Pale conspiracy—

moonlit ravens' cobalt glow:

artificial snow

Timeless poetry is born of solitude and sacrifice. Embrace adversity; find joy in trials. Delight in every dark, difficult moment.

Moonlight refracted,

a whisper of winter wind—

life's blizzards begin

Cabin solitaire—

applewood fire glows garnet;

wolves howl in my woods

Quietus Est

Obscure, botanical eclipse:
nightshade's starry sepal skies—
she kisses toxic, lust-stained lips;
quietus est, and daily dies.

LIGHT FRAMES THE FOREST

Deep in my mind's caves,

dire wolves shadow my spirit—

fire through nightmare eyes

Ravens hold vigil,

as corpse-green fog settles low,

thick on frosty ponds

Shallow, frosted breath—

twilight beckons lady death;

snow falls softly now

My Apocalypse

Nothing remains; I see
only sicariidae—
venomous, brown, six-eyed spiders
creep across the empty quarter,
an abandoned sector of dust:
my burnt, barren space.

Nothing remains; I hear
our collective drunkenness
repeat the hollow Internet refrains
of deceptive politicians, nihilistic poets,
and avaricious influencers:
my buried, beneath nuclear waste.

Nothing remains; I respire
vapors of putrefied, white-hot flesh,
their lethal ashes scorch tired lungs;
molten asphalt crater,
piled high with charred corpses:
my rubble home.

Nothing remains; I sense
still intersections, blank streetlights,
noonday, dark as death,
a deep, deafening, silent scream—
the quiet of desolation:
end of my nation.

Nothing remains; I plead,
"But why?
Is this all there is, God,
loneliness, isolation?"
I take a measured breath,
and die: my repose, or ruination.

Death's haunting shadow

darts about pine coffin walls:

darkest solitude

Even love poems succumb to the way of all earth.

Peace doesn't begin on the battlefield;
it begins in homes and neighborhoods,
and in the hearts and minds of individuals.

He brings peace.
He is peace.

When hearts and minds are one,
and there are no poor among us,
peace will reign.

Late candlelight quests,

searching wet cobblestone streets—

lonely pathways home

The By and By

Death's sweeping sickle draws out lies;
her pale moon haunts sepulchral skies.
I see through dimly veiled eyes;
I see her hollow, spectral guise—

In the by and by
In the by and by

Dust to dust, all creatures die;
ash to ash, their spirits fly.
May we dwell in the by and by;
again embrace, again, there cry—

In the by and by
In the by and by

Stand, brave bison king!

Fight fiercely, Great Plains warrior!

Rise with the white sun.

Of Light and Life

Time streams through death's glass;
sands dance as hours pass.
All time ends in sorrow.
All time is but borrowed.

Time fills my hourglass;
time waits beyond my grasp.
Time slips into the past.
Time slips into the past.

Time drains our dark souls;
fallen hearts are time's fools.
Deep beneath death's dank soil,
our shells rot of life's toil.

Time waits and slyly laughs;
sands dance as years pass.
Death fills life's fragile glass.
Death fills life's fragile glass.

Wake from the black abyss,
raised now by Our Lord's kiss.
Rise, my jewel of the dead;
all words we say, we've said.

Remember love, we will be,
when futures we don't yet see,
in some far, distant place,
like our pasts, beyond light's gate.

Light fills our hourglass;
light flows within our grasp.
Death slips into the past.
Death slips into the past.

LIGHT FRAMES THE FOREST

*Too few women read classic works of literature;
too few men read.*

*There's nothing better than a book.
The best books are poetry, and Holy Writ.*

Huck's Psalm

Life's storms descend each day,
they knock me from my feet;
with trembling tears, and fears,
this surge, I rise to meet.

Father, I'm swept away,
dashed down upon the docks—
relentless, rough waters,
swift rivers, jagged rocks.

Crushed by worldly currents,
I pray peace from above;
you guide me to a brook
of gentle, endless love.

Warm winds soothe my spirit,
still pools calm my heart;
ahead the rapids rage
to rip my soul apart.

Lightning bolts, thunderclaps,
tempted, and torn by grief—
head bloodied, but not bowed,
again, I seek relief.

Your soft voice speaks wisdom
on wings of snowy dove,
invites me to swim the stream
of everlasting love.

Winter's near; I'm going;
like the cool brook, I flow.
Life's tempests weren't easy,
but through them I did grow.

I thank thee, Heavenly Father,
for now I sense the end;
you reach down across your kingdom
and lift me home, again.

By Norman "Huck" Watson

My love, what remains

at day's end, starry nightfall,

is eternal peace

Luces Peruanas

(Peruvian Lights)

The Nazca Lines

From river Sidon
they walked the Bountiful line
to the west seashore—

a day and a half's
journey between Bountiful
and Desolation.

A pathway across
Nazca's narrow neck of land?
A border of shells?

Who laid the measures?
Who stretched the lines upon it?
Ghost trails in the sand—

Sun Gems

(hummingbirds and angels)

Towers of crisp vines
delineate sacred shapes
around muddy pools—

Sky kings, seraphim,
Andean bearers of light,
drink nectars' knowledge;

Watchers descend from
Celestial spheres: God's angels
sent forth to protect.

Liahona: Light of Paracas?

"To God is the Guidance"

I watched an Incan fisherman
sketch wisdom in the low-tide sand—
like the geoglyphs at Nazca,
mysteries drawn by ancient hands.

I pondered the Candelabra's glow
on the mountainside at dusk.
Did dry winds of the Sechura
whisper scripture out of thy dust?

Humble people of Paracas,
wandering barks beneath the stars—
Liahona, shining compass,
brass reflection of faithful hearts

I dreamed of civilizations
where petrified sands fell like rain
and conquerors rode waves of lust,
tempest-tossed from the shores of Spain.

Prayerful people of Paracas,
forever know God's guiding ways—
Was Liahona, true compass,
carved in rock over Pisco Bay?

Writing poetry is a solitary, introspective endeavor. Ofttimes my poetry is only for me; it's what I need to say, and I need to say it in writing. My devotional poems are personally sacred words I recite to myself. I've rarely felt compelled to publish or explain them.

I write poetry because it enriches my life. It fills my soul with light, His light. And I pray that His light touches and inspires others through my work.

The central theme of my poetry is a single existential question: "Is this all there is?" To which my answer is an emphatic, unapologetic, "No."

His light defines me. His light frames the forest.

Et lux in tenebris lucet.

About the Author

S.C. Watson is a prize-winning poet and writer residing in Westminster, Colorado. He holds a BA degree in English from Brigham Young University and a JD degree from Willamette University College of Law. He is co-owner of Baja Bad Press, a small, family-run publishing company, and the author of *Christmas Coventry at Fool Hollow* (International Book Awards, finalist, 2023) and *Baja Bad* (2020). He is also the originator of HaiX (chiastic haiku), an original form of poetry.

He has traveled throughout Mexico, South America, and Europe, and speaks fluent Spanish. He attributes his creative writing training to his studies under renowned Welsh poet Leslie Norris and American writer Bruce W. Jorgensen.

He is married to talented artist, photographer, and poet Andréa Watson, who illustrates their books and is co-owner of their publishing company. They can be contacted at BajaBadPress@gmail.com.

www.ingramcontent.com/pod-product-compliance
Lightning Source LLC
Chambersburg PA
CBHW030556080526
44585CB00012B/396